J. WESTON
WALCH
PUBLISHER

FOCUS ON
READING

Ella Enchanted

LISA
FRENCH

User's Guide
to
Walch Reproducible Books

Purchasers of this book are granted the right to reproduce all pages.

This permission is limited to a single teacher, for classroom use only.

Any questions regarding this policy or requests to purchase further reproduction rights should be addressed to

Permissions Editor
J. Weston Walch, Publisher
321 Valley Street • P.O. Box 658
Portland, Maine 04104-0658

1   2   3   4   5   6   7   8   9   10
ISBN 0-8251-4600-3
Copyright © 2003
J. Weston Walch, Publisher
P. O. Box 658 • Portland, Maine 04104-0658
walch.com
Printed in the United States of America

Contents

Introduction/Classroom Management . . . . *iv*
Focus on the Book . . . . *vi*

Focus Your Knowledge 1

I. CHAPTERS ONE–FIVE
Focus Your Reading 2–3
Build Your Vocabulary 4
Check Your Understanding:
  Multiple Choice 5
Check Your Understanding:
  Short Answer 6
Deepen Your Understanding 7

II. CHAPTERS SIX–TEN
Focus Your Reading 8–9
Build Your Vocabulary 10
Check Your Understanding:
  Multiple Choice 11
Check Your Understanding:
  Short Answer 12
Deepen Your Understanding 13

III. CHAPTERS ELEVEN–FIFTEEN
Focus Your Reading 14–15
Build Your Vocabulary 16
Check Your Understanding:
  Multiple Choice 17
Check Your Understanding:
  Short Answer 18
Deepen Your Understanding 19

IV. CHAPTERS SIXTEEN–TWENTY
Focus Your Reading 20–21
Build Your Vocabulary 22
Check Your Understanding:
  Multiple Choice 23
Check Your Understanding:
  Short Answer 24
Deepen Your Understanding 25

V. CHAPTERS TWENTY-ONE–TWENTY-FIVE
Focus Your Reading 26–27
Build Your Vocabulary 28
Check Your Understanding:
  Multiple Choice 29
Check Your Understanding:
  Short Answer 30
Deepen Your Understanding 31

VI. CHAPTERS TWENTY-SIX–EPILOGUE
Focus Your Reading 32–33
Build Your Vocabulary 34
Check Your Understanding:
  Multiple Choice 35
Check Your Understanding:
  Short Answer 36
Deepen Your Understanding 37

End-of-Book Test 38
Answer Key 40

WELCOME TO *FOCUS ON READING*

Focus on Reading literature study guides are designed to help all students comprehend and analyze their reading. Many teachers have grappled with the question of how to make quality literature accessible to all students. Students who are already avid readers of quality literature are motivated to read and are familiar with prereading and reading strategies. However, struggling readers frequently lack basic reading skills and are not equipped with the prior knowledge and reading strategies to thoroughly engage in the classroom literature experience.

Focus on Reading is designed to make teachers' and students' lives easier! How? By providing materials that allow all students to take part in reading quality literature. Each *Focus on Reading* study guide contains activities that focus on vocabulary and comprehension skills that students need to get the most from their reading. In addition, each section within the guide contains a before-reading **Focus Your Reading** page containing tools to ensure success: **Vocabulary Words to Know, Things to Know,** and **Questions to Think About.** These study aids will help students who may not have the prior knowledge they need to truly comprehend the reading.

USING *FOCUS ON READING*

Focus on Reading is designed to make it easy for you to meet the individual needs of students who require additional reading skills support. Each *Focus on Reading* study guide contains teacher and student support materials, reproducible student activity sheets, an end-of-book test, and an answer key.

- **Focus on the Book,** a convenient reference section for the teacher, provides a brief overview of the entire book including a synopsis, information about the setting, author data, and historical background.

- **Focus Your Knowledge,** a reference page for students, is a whole-book, prereading activity designed to activate prior knowledge and immerse students in the topic.

The study guide divides the novel into 6 manageable sections to make it easy to plan classroom time. Five activities are devoted to each section of the novel.

Before Reading

- **Focus Your Reading** consists of 3 prereading sections:

Vocabulary Words to Know lists and defines 10 vocabulary words students will encounter in their reading. Students will not have to interrupt their reading to look up, ask for, or spend a lot of time figuring out the meaning of unfamiliar words. These words are later studied in-depth within the lesson.

Things to Know identifies terms or concepts that are integral to the reading but that may not be familiar to today's students. This section is intended to "level the playing field" for those students who may not have much prior knowledge about the time period, culture, or theme of the book. It also gets students involved with the book, increasing interest before they begin reading.

Questions to Think About helps students focus on the main ideas and important details they should be looking for as they read. This activity helps give students a *purpose* for reading. The goal of these guiding questions is to build knowledge, confidence, and comfort with the topics in the reading.

During Reading

- **Build Your Vocabulary** presents the 10 unit focus words in the exact context of the book. Students are then asked to write their own definitions and sentences for the words.

- **Check Your Understanding: Multiple Choice** offers 10 multiple-choice, literal comprehension questions for each section.

- **Check Your Understanding: Short Answer** contains 10 short-answer questions based on the reading.

After Reading

- **Deepen Your Understanding** is a writing activity that extends appreciation and analysis of the book. This activity focuses on critical-thinking skills and literary analysis.

- **End-of-Book Test** contains 20 multiple-choice items covering the book. These items ask questions that require students to synthesize the information in the book and make inferences in their answers.

CLASSROOM MANAGEMENT

Focus on Reading is very flexible. It can be used by the whole class, by small groups, or by individuals. Each study guide divides the novel into 6 manageable units of study.

This literature comprehension program is simple to use. Just photocopy the lessons and distribute them at the appropriate time as students read the novel.

You may want to reproduce and discuss the **Focus Your Knowledge** page before distributing the paperbacks. This page develops and activates prior knowledge to ensure that students have a grounding in the book before beginning reading. After reading this whole-book prereading page, students are ready to dive into the book.

The **Focus Your Reading** prereading activities are the keystone of this program. They prepare students for what they are going to read, providing focus for the complex task of reading. These pages should be distributed before students actually begin reading the corresponding section of the novel. There are no questions to be answered on these pages; these are for reference and support during reading. Students may choose to take notes on these pages as they read. This will also give students a study tool for review before the **End-of-Book Test.**

The **Focus Your Reading** pages also provide an excellent bridge to home. Parents, mentors, tutors, or other involved adults can review vocabulary words with students, offer their own insights about the historical and cultural background outlined, and become familiar with the ideas students will be reading about. This can help families talk to students in a meaningful way about their reading, and it gives the adults something concrete to ask about to be sure that students are reading and understanding.

The **Build Your Vocabulary** and **Check Your Understanding: Multiple Choice** and **Short Answer** activities should be distributed when students begin reading the corresponding section of the novel. These literature guide pages are intended to help students comprehend and retain what they read; they should be available for students to refer to at any time during the reading.

Deepen Your Understanding is an optional extension activity that goes beyond literal questions about the book, asking students for their own ideas and opinions—and the reasons behind them. These postreading activities generally focus on literary analysis.

As reflected in its title, the **End-of-Book Test** is a postreading comprehension test to be completed after the entire novel has been read.

For your convenience, a clear **Answer Key** simplifies the scoring process.

Focus on the Book

Synopsis

Ella of Frell has a life that many other young women might envy: wealthy parents, a comfortable manor for a home, a life of leisure, and the loving attention of Mandy, the cook—who also happens to be her fairy godmother. Unfortunately, Ella has a secret that only her mother and Mandy know. She has been cursed at birth by the "blessing" of a well-meaning but foolish fairy named Lucinda; the gift is total obedience. For nearly fifteen years, Ella has resisted the curse in her own small way, but its power is overwhelming. She is obliged to obey anyone who gives her an order, no matter how foolish, or even dangerous, the consequences. Finding the careless Lucinda and persuading her to reverse the curse becomes one of Ella's chief aims in life.

When Ella's beloved mother dies suddenly, her life takes an unsettling turn. While Sir Peter, her mercenary father, calculates remarriage to rich, vulgar Dame Olga, he sends Ella off to finishing school with Dame Olga's two unpleasant daughters. At Madame Edith's establishment, Ella is forced to become an "accomplished" young lady—learning against her will to embroider, dance, sing, and even eat with daintiness and grace.

When Ella learns that her father will be attending a giant's wedding in a country to the north, she realizes that Lucinda the fairy may also be one of the wedding guests. On the chance of meeting her, Ella runs away from school and heads north on foot. On the way, she is treated with great hospitality in the kingdom of the elves but is later captured by a band of hungry, carnivorous ogres. In the nick of time, Ella is rescued by Prince Charmont, son of the king and queen of Frell, and his band of knights. Ella and Char are already acquainted; their friendship now grows stronger.

Escorted by one of Char's knights, Ella arrives in the land of the giants in time to witness the wedding. She finds Lucinda but has no luck convincing her to end the curse. In the meantime, Father spots Ella in the crowd and is struck by her newly acquired "feminine" charms. Admitting that he has lost all of his money, he takes Ella home and prepares to marry her off to a suitably wealthy man. When his first attempt fails, Father decides to marry himself off instead—to Dame Olga.

Ella's life takes yet another downturn when her father remarries then sets off on a long business trip. Left to the devices of her greedy, heartless stepmother and stepsisters, Ella is forced to become the most menial of servants. She is ordered about from dawn until dark and thwarted in any attempts to communicate with Char. At last, however, Ella's fortune turns. Three royal balls are held in order to introduce the prince to possible consorts. With the help of Mandy—and even a reformed Lucinda—Ella attends the balls, captures the prince's heart once more, and lives happily ever after. This updated take on the classic *Cinderella* story thus comes to a satisfying close.

About the Author

Gail Carson Levine was born in 1947 in New York City. Influenced by parents who were committed to both education and the arts, she began to write and paint at an early age. As an adult, Levine pursued painting while earning her living as a social worker. A budding interest in illustrating children's books, however, eventually led to a passion for writing such books herself. Levine enrolled in a writing class; it was there that she came up with her idea to retell the Cinderella story:

> I had to write something for class, and I couldn't think of a plot. The fairy tale "Cinderella" already had a plot, so I decided to do a Cinderella story. Then, when I thought about Cinderella's character, I realized she was such a goody two-shoes that I would hate her before I finished ten pages. So I came up with the curse: she's only good because she has to be, and she's in constant rebellion.

This class project became *Ella Enchanted*, Levine's first novel. Published in 1997, it became an immediate success, winning a Newbery Honor, an ALA Best Book for Young Adults, and other awards.

Since the publication of *Ella Enchanted*, Levine has devoted her time to writing. Her more recent works include *Dave at Night* (1999), *The Wish* (1999), *The Fairy's Mistake* (1999), *Princess Sonora and the Long Sleep* (1999), *Cinderellis and the Glass Hill* (2000), and *Two Princesses of Bamarre* (2001).

(continued)

Historical Background

Since this novel is a fantasy, its setting is only loosely based on historic fact. Although the presence of manors and chivalrous knights would place the story in northern Europe during the late Middle Ages, the range of Renaissance dances performed at court suggest the sixteenth, or even seventeenth, century. In this case, historical accuracy is of lesser importance than the novel's basis in the fairy tale tradition.

Ella Enchanted is, first and foremost, a retelling of the classic Cinderella story from a late-twentieth-century perspective. Ella, a highly intelligent young woman with an independent, creative spirit, is contrasted sharply with her more traditional, stereotypically feminine peers. Ella is obedient only because a fairy's curse literally forces her to be. Her classmates, on the other hand, are obedient because they believe that submission and docility are the only appropriate "female" behavior. While Olive and Hattie, Ella's odious stepsisters, are grooming themselves for wealthy husbands, Ella is interested in foreign languages and seeing the world.

Ella's belief—and Prince Charmont's—in a marriage based on love (a romantic tradition with Renaissance roots) is juxtaposed against her classmates', and her own father's, belief in marriage as a tool for social and economic gain.

Ella also represents a more democratic, less class-conscious view of the Western world. While Hattie and Olive shun Ella's friend Areida because her innkeeping family is of a lower rank, Ella is able to look beyond the restrictions of an outmoded class system to befriend someone who is fun-loving and kindhearted.

Throughout the novel, there are references to many other well-known fairy tales, including *Sleeping Beauty, The Shoemaker and the Elves, Beauty and the Beast, Aladdin, Hansel and Gretel,* and *Rapunzel.* There are frequent incidents involving giants, ogres, elves, gnomes, and other fantastic or mythological creatures. In most cases, the author has used a "fractured fairy tale" approach that addresses these creatures of myth and legend with great humor and insight.

Focus Your Knowledge

Every book you read belongs to a particular genre, or class, of literature. For example, you might choose to read a mystery over a romance. Other people prefer poetry, biographies or autobiographies, historical fiction, or "how-to-do-it" books.

Do you remember any folktales or fairy tales? Most people are familiar with Snow White, Jack and the Beanstalk, Goldilocks and the Three Bears, and other colorful characters from the fictional world. In fact, folk- and fairy tales belong to the literary genre known as *fantasy*. A fantasy is a story in which fanciful, impossible things happen. Strange creatures, such as giants, ogres, and imps, make trouble for helpless humans, and magical creatures like fairies and elves clean up the mess. In most cases, the hero or heroine lives "happily ever after."

• Think of some familiar fairy tales. In what time and place is each one set? Can you always tell what the specific setting is? Why or why not?

• What kinds of creatures appear in these stories? What special powers—for good or for evil—do they possess?

• Now think of the heroes and heroines of these tales. What strengths and weaknesses do these characters have? What special dilemmas do they face? How do they solve their problems? How much "outside" help do they need?

One of the most famous fairy tales of all time is *Cinderella.* The Cinderella story, in fact, is told all over the world in over a thousand different versions. The version that we know, however, is a blend of a French fairy tale (written down by Charles Perrault in 1697) and a German tale (recorded by the Brothers Grimm in 1812). In the novel *Ella Enchanted,* you will read yet another version of the Cinderella story—one in which the heroine is a little bit different.

• As you read, compare Ella of Frell with the traditional Cinderella. How do they differ?

Focus Your Reading

Vocabulary Words to Know

Study the following words and definitions. You will meet these words in your reading. Be sure to jot down in your word journal any other unknown words from the reading.

inconsolably—in a manner showing that the subject cannot be comforted

docile—easily managed or taught; obedient

allegiance—loyalty; duty to one's lord or ruler

gesturing—moving the body to express or emphasize an idea

avidly—eagerly; greedily

complacently—in a self-satisfied manner

voluminous—having great volume or bulk; very large or full

faceted—having cleanly cut surfaces that are smooth and flat

severed—cut in two

hapless—unlucky; unfortunate

Things to Know

Here is some background information about this section of the book.

Marchpane is another word for *marzipan*, a sweet made of finely crushed almonds, sugar, and egg whites.

The **battering ram** was used in medieval times to break down the doors and walls of castles and other large buildings. A battering ram usually consisted of a large wooden beam or pole with an iron head. It was held by a team of men and rammed, head first, into the target.

Courtiers served their king or queen at the royal court. They often spoke to flatter or impress their ruler rather than to tell the truth.

A **manor** was a large house located on a feudal estate during the Middle Ages. The owners of the estate lived in the manor house and were usually titled (*Lord, Lady, Earl,* and so on).

A **high chancellor** was the chief secretary of the king or queen.

Focus Your Reading

Questions to Think About

The following questions will help you understand the meaning of what you read. You do not have to write out the answers to these questions. Instead, look at them before you begin reading, and think about them while you are reading.

1. What clues in the text suggest the time and place in which this novel is set?

2. What details in the text add to the fantasy element in the story?

3. How does the author contrast Ella's relationship with her mother to Ella's relationship with her father?

4. What examples in the text begin to reveal Ella's character?

5. What happens when Ella tries to resist an order?

Build Your Vocabulary

Read the sentences below. On the line, write your definition of the word in bold type. Then, on another sheet of paper, use that word in a new sentence of your own.

1. "When I cried **inconsolably** through my first hour of life, my tears were her inspiration."
   inconsolably: _____

2. "Instead of making me **docile,** Lucinda's curse made a rebel of me."
   docile: _____

3. "Part of the speech had been about dying, but more was about giving **allegiance** to Kyrria and its rulers. . . ."
   allegiance: _____

4. " 'Cousin of mine,' the prince said, **gesturing** at the tombstone."
   gesturing: _____

5. "Then she'd tuck in again, as **avidly** as ever."
   avidly: _____

6. "Hattie smiled **complacently.**"
   complacently: _____

7. "I had trouble sitting down at the table because Bertha had made me wear a fashionable gown, and my petticoat was **voluminous.**"
   voluminous: _____

8. "In front of his plate was a many-**faceted** crystal goblet."
   faceted: _____

9. "It fell and broke neatly into two pieces, stem **severed** from body."
   severed: _____

10. "When the spring was released, the fist shot out at a **hapless** puppet."
    hapless: _____

Check Your Understanding

Multiple Choice

Circle the letter of the best answer to each question.

1. What "gift" does Lucinda give to Ella shortly after Ella's birth?
   a. curiosity
   b. obedience
   c. language ability

2. What command does Mother give after Ella punches Pamela in the nose?
   a. She orders Ella never to tell about the curse.
   b. She orders Ella never to use violence.
   c. She orders Mandy to make curing soup.

3. How does Father's palm feel to Mandy when they hold hands at the funeral?
   a. cool and scaly
   b. cold and clammy
   c. moist and hot

4. How did Prince Charmont learn of Ella?
   a. Ella's mother told him at a party.
   b. Ella's cook talked to the prince's cook.
   c. The king spied on Ella and her family.

5. What does Ella put on when she and her father return from Mother's funeral?
   a. an embroidered black mourning dress
   b. a dress of dove gray and scarlet
   c. a dress of spicy green

6. What does Ella find "disgusting to watch" when Dame Olga and her daughters pay their respects?
   a. Dame Olga's flirtation with her father
   b. the way Hattie and Olive eat
   c. Hattie's method of counting all the windows in Ella's manor

7. Why, in Mandy's opinion, has Ella's mother died?
   a. She took the unicorn hair out of her bowl of curing soup.
   b. She went out too often and didn't get enough rest.
   c. Ella's father has been too cruel.

8. When Ella's father first talks about finishing school, what reason does he give?
   a. He wants her to not walk like an elephant.
   b. He wants her to learn enough to help him with his business.
   c. He hopes that she will become much better friends with Hattie and Olga.

9. How does Father respond when Ella says he can hire a governess instead of sending her to finishing school?
   a. There are no suitable governesses in the kingdom.
   b. He is afraid Ella would be too lonely at home with a governess.
   c. A governess would be much more expensive than finishing school.

10. What two gifts does Mandy give Ella before leaving for finishing school?
    a. a necklace and a pair of slippers
    b. a book of fairy tales and a little porcelain castle
    c. a necklace and a book of fairy tales

Check Your Understanding

Short Answer

Write a short answer for each question.

1. At what age, and under what circumstances, does Ella first learn that she has been cursed?

2. What does Ella remember as she walks down the spiral staircase when Mother is ill?

3. What does Father do when Ella begins to cry at her mother's funeral?

4. What happens when Char hands Ella into the carriage after the funeral, and how does Char respond?

5. What does Ella experience when she tries to resist her father's order to change her clothes after the funeral?

6. What does Hattie tell Ella about Father when the two girls first meet?

7. When Ella asks Mandy about the unusual carpet in the hall, what does Ella learn about Mandy herself?

8. According to Mandy, how has Ella already begun to show that she has some fairy blood?

9. How does Mandy respond when Ella asks her to help break Lucinda's spell?

10. When Father is angry, of what kind of toy does Ella say he reminds her, and why?

Deepen Your Understanding

"That fool of a fairy Lucinda did not intend to lay a curse on me. She meant to bestow a gift."

—*Chapter One*

The first two sentences of *Ella Enchanted,* quoted above, do a good job of "grabbing" the reader's attention. This is a *strong opening.* It captures our interest and makes us want to keep reading to find out more. In fact, an author's opening lines are critical in setting the tone, theme, or central conflict of a story. Answer the following questions about the first lines of the book.

• How do the two opening lines reveal key information about the rest of the book?

• What tone does the author create through her specific choice of words?

Focus Your Reading

Vocabulary Words to Know

Study the following words and definitions. You will meet these words in your reading. Be sure to jot down in your word journal any other unknown words from the reading.

menagerie—a collection of wild or exotic animals that can be visited and viewed

ferocity—fierceness; violence

disdainful—looking down one's nose; scornful

relished—enjoyed greatly

diversion—something that draws one's attention away from the present situation

prosperous—successful; enjoying good fortune

succumb—to give in; to die

stupor—a dazed state that can be caused by extreme stress

epithets—abusive words addressed to other people

ciphering—arithmetic; mathematical calculations

Things to Know

Here is some background information about this section of the book.

A **bailiff** is an assistant to a British sheriff. Bailiffs can serve people with official legal notices, including arrest warrants. In the Middle Ages, they could even carry out executions.

A **hydra** was a snakelike monster from Greek mythology. A hydra had many heads.

A **gryphon** (or griffin) was a creature from folklore that was half eagle, half lion.

A **centaur** was another creature from Greek mythology. It was half man, half horse.

Focus Your Reading

Questions to Think About

The following questions will help you understand the meaning of what you read. You do not have to write out the answers to these questions. Instead, look at them before you begin reading, and think about them while you are reading.

1. How does Ella's second meeting with Prince Charmont at the menagerie affect their budding friendship?

2. How might Ella's foreign-language skills prove helpful in the world beyond the manor?

3. What does the mother gnome see in Ella's future? What does she particularly warn Ella about?

4. How does the journey to school affect Ella's relationships with both Hattie and Olive?

5. What subjects are taught at Madame Edith's school? Why are these considered important?

Build Your Vocabulary

Read the sentences below. On the line, write your definition of the word in bold type. Then, on another sheet of paper, use that word in a new sentence of your own.

1. " . . . I started for the royal **menagerie** just outside the walls of the king's palace. My favorite exhibits were the talking birds and the exotic animals."
   menagerie: _____

2. "[The baby dragon] was beautiful in his tiny **ferocity** and seemed happiest when flaming, his ruby eyes gleaming evilly."
   ferocity: _____

3. "He wasn't haughty or **disdainful,** or stuffy, as High Chancellor Thomas was."
   disdainful: _____

4. "And then I **relished** her nauseated expression when she swallowed."
   relished: _____

5. "I stared out the window at a flock of sheep and wished for a **diversion** that would take my mind away from lamb and lentil salad."
   diversion: _____

6. "Except for its enormous ornamental shrubs pruned into the shapes of wide-skirted maidens, it might have been the home of any not-so-**prosperous** merchant."
   prosperous: _____

7. "If I didn't **succumb** to starvation, I would be here for a long time, with hateful mistresses and with Hattie ordering me about."
   succumb: _____

8. "I stared out the window at Madame Edith's garden until exhaustion and hunger produced a kind of **stupor** in me."
   stupor: _____

9. "I didn't know any insults in Ayorthaian. However, Areida was laughing, which made it seem the worst of **epithets.**"
   epithets: _____

10. "The only subjects that came easily were those taught by Writing Mistress: composition and **ciphering.**"
    ciphering: _____

Check Your Understanding

Multiple Choice

Circle the letter of the best answer to each question.

1. What does Ella do when she visits the dragon at the menagerie?
   a. She accidentally lets it out of its cage.
   b. She speaks to it in a special language.
   c. She toasts some cheese in its flames.

2. Why does Ella try to break her curse at the menagerie?
   a. She does not want Char to order her around.
   b. She thinks the centaur will command her to do something dangerous.
   c. The ogre orders her to come closer with the young gnome.

3. What do the Gnomic words mean that Ella uses to calm the young gnome?
   a. "Every gnome likes to be at home."
   b. "Digging is good for the wealth and good for the health."
   c. "Early to bed and early to rise makes a gnome healthy, wealthy, and wise."

4. What does Hattie get Ella to do during the coach ride to school?
   a. She makes Ella give her the silver necklace from Ella's mother.
   b. She makes Ella give her all of her KJs.
   c. She tells Ella to sit with the coachman.

5. What does Hattie see when she demands to look at Ella's book of fairy tales?
   a. information about centaur ticks and gnomish mining
   b. "The Shoemaker and the Elves"
   c. a map of Frell and a picture of Sir Peter

6. Why does Ella eat only a bite of bread for breakfast on the trip to school?
   a. Traveling makes her stomach ill.
   b. Hattie orders her not to eat.
   c. She is afraid of looking as greedy as Hattie and Olive.

7. How does Ella help break the spell cast by the ogres' voices on the way to school?
   a. She tells everyone in the coach to start yelling so that they cannot hear them.
   b. She speaks to them in their language, asking them to go away in peace.
   c. She helps the coachman whip the horses into a faster gallop.

8. How does Sewing Mistress punish Ella for sewing three messy stitches in one hour?
   a. She makes her stay after class to do the work over again more neatly.
   b. She rips the stitches out and tells her to do one hundred neat stitches.
   c. She sends Ella away without supper.

9. Not including Ella, how many girls sleep in Ella's bedroom at school?
   a. four
   b. five
   c. six

10. Why does Ella not excel at penmanship?
    a. She finds it boring.
    b. Hattie orders her not to do her best.
    c. Writing Mistress never gives orders.

Check Your Understanding

Short Answer

Write a short answer for each question.

1. What kinds of creatures live in the royal menagerie?

2. According to Ella, in what ways are ogres dangerous?

3. How does Char get Ella to stop moving toward the ogre?

4. What does Ella do when Hattie orders her to pick up the dust in the carriage?

5. When Olive demands a present from Ella in the carriage, what does Ella give her?

6. Why does Hattie allow Ella to drink Tonic on the trip to school?

7. What finally makes Olive stop screaming after the ogres disappear from sight?

8. How does Ella look when she first arrives at school and joins the embroidery lesson?

9. How do Ella and Areida communicate when they do not want anyone else to listen?

10. According to Mandy's letter, what has the prince brought Ella as a gift?

Deepen Your Understanding

"Whenever I had time, I practiced the languages, especially Ogrese. The meanings were dreadful, but there was an attraction in speaking the words. They were smooth, sleek, and slithery, the way a talking snake would sound."

–Chapter Ten

In these sentences from *Ella Enchanted,* the author uses a powerful literary device called *alliteration.* Alliteration means repeating the same consonant sound at the beginning of two or more neighboring words.

Alliteration helps to create a clearer picture in the reader's mind. It reinforces a key image or feeling. In the example above, Gail Carson Levine uses alliteration to call up both the image and the sound of a snake. The snake imagery goes along with Ella's description of the "dreadful" language of the ogres.

Write a paragraph about one of the characters or creatures in *Ella Enchanted.* Include alliteration in at least two different sentences.

Focus Your Reading

Vocabulary Words to Know

Study the following words and definitions. You will meet these words in your reading. Be sure to jot down in your word journal any other unknown words from the reading.

condescension—a superior air

odious—hateful; disgusting

devise—to invent

posturing—posing; acting in an affected manner to impress someone

skirmish—a small fight

paltry—inferior; trivial

vouchsafed—granted or given graciously

woebegone—miserable; sorrowful

convulsively—with abnormally strong contraction of the muscles; violently

biddable—easily controlled or taught

Things to Know

Here is some background information about this section of the book.

A **topiary** is a group of trees or shrubs that are cut and trimmed into special ornamental shapes.

The **phoenix** was a legendary bird that lived for hundreds of years, burned itself up, and then rose from its ashes to live again.

A **stirrup** cup was a cup that was offered with a farewell drink to someone leaving on horseback.

Knights were an important part of feudal society during the Middle Ages. They worked and fought for the lord and lady of the manor to whom they swore their loyalty.

Focus Your Reading

Questions to Think About

The following questions will help you understand the meaning of what you read. You do not have to write out the answers to these questions. Instead, look at them before you begin reading, and think about them while you are reading.

1. How well does Ella relate to the other girls at school? How well does she relate to her teachers? Why?

2. What techniques does Ella use to resist feeling "like a complete puppet" because of her curse?

3. How does Ella's friendship with Areida affect Ella's experiences at school, both positively and negatively?

4. How do Dame Olga's goals for her daughters reflect the social attitudes of her time? How well does Ella reflect these ideals?

5. What role does Ella's magic book from Mandy play in this novel? How does Ella use her intelligence to use the information she gets from the book?

Build Your Vocabulary

Read the sentences below. On the line, write your definition of the word in bold type. Then, on another sheet of paper, use that word in a new sentence of your own.

1. "... they treated me with the same oily **condescension** Hattie visited on me in public."
   condescension: _____

2. "They were an **odious** group, Hattie and the two she called her special friends, Blossom and Delicia."
   odious: _____

3. "Hattie's orders were chiefly chores. I think she lacked the imagination to **devise** more interesting commands."
   devise: _____

4. "She stopped to pick a flower and lift it to her nose, **posturing** for me."
   posturing: _____

5. " 'Perhaps the ogres will raid and there will be a **skirmish.**' "
   skirmish: _____

6. " 'It is a great distance to go to learn such **paltry** tricks.' "
   paltry: _____

7. "Frantically, I riffled the pages of my book, hoping to be **vouchsafed** a map."
   vouchsafed: _____

8. "I loved his howl, which I could both hear and feel: long and plaintive, **woebegone** and heartsore ..."
   woebegone: _____

9. "I swallowed **convulsively.** My stomach heaved and I threw up."
   convulsively: _____

10. " 'The young lady can tell them [the ogres] to go wherever we say. . . . She can come with us and keep them **biddable.**' "
    biddable: _____

Check Your Understanding

Multiple Choice

Circle the letter of the best answer to each question.

1. After smelling the bogweed, what does Hattie tell Ella that amazes her?
   a. She says that she wants to be Ella's friend.
   b. She says that she prefers Ella to Olive.
   c. She says that Ella is pretty and brave.

2. What order does Hattie give Ella after seeing Ella and Areida giggling in the hall?
   a. Hattie tells Ella to end their friendship.
   b. Hattie says that Areida and Ella must include her in their group, too.
   c. Hattie says that Ella must steal money and jewelry from Areida.

3. After reading Dame Olga's letter in her magic book, what does Ella figure out about Hattie and Dame Olga?
   a. They are both secretly engaged.
   b. They both want Olive's money.
   c. They both wear wigs.

4. Where does Ella discover that Father is going on October 15?
   a. to the wedding of Uaaxee's daughter
   b. to the elves' forest to trade with Slannen
   c. to ask Dame Olga to marry him

5. What does Ella do with Hattie's wig after she runs away from school?
   a. She throws it into the moat.
   b. She trades it for muffins and bread.
   c. She gives it to the elf woman.

6. What gift does Slannen give Ella before she leaves the land of the elves?
   a. a cup in the shape of a wolf's head and shoulders
   b. a dragon-shaped coal scuttle
   c. a nut dish in the shape of a centaur

7. What happens to the pony that the elves lend Ella for her trip?
   a. It runs away after the ogres grab Ella.
   b. The ogres eat it.
   c. Ella commands it to run and fetch help.

8. How does Ella avoid being eaten by the ogres?
   a. She trades the pottery from the elves.
   b. The elves rescue her and kill the ogres.
   c. She speaks to them in Ogrese and lulls them to sleep.

9. How do Char and his knights avoid being overpowered by the ogres' spell?
   a. They talk and laugh very loudly so that they drown out the ogres' voices.
   b. They speak in Ogrese and charm the ogres into thinking they are all friends.
   c. They put beeswax in their ears so that they can't hear the ogres' voices.

10. How does Char help Ella reach the giant's wedding?
    a. He has Sir Stephan serve as her escort.
    b. He gives her a new pony to replace the one that she has lost.
    c. He calls for the centaur to carry her.

Check Your Understanding

Short Answer

Write a short answer for each question.

1. How well does Ella get along with the mistresses and the other girls at school?

2. What effect does Areida's singing of the Ayorthaian mourning song have on Ella?

3. According to Dame Olga's letter, what things will make her daughters "fine ladies"?

4. Why does Ella decide to try to attend the wedding of Uaaxee's daughter?

5. How does the baker show Ella the way to the land of the giants?

6. Why does Ella say that her first two days on the road after running away are the best since before Mother died?

7. Why do the elves trust Ella even though they dislike her father?

8. Why is Ella unable to get away from the ogres' camp even when all of the ogres are sleeping soundly?

9. How do Char and his knights know where Ella and the ogres are?

10. Why does Char blush?

Deepen Your Understanding

At Madame Edith's finishing school, young ladies are taught basic reading, writing, and arithmetic. They also are taught to sew with very small stitches, to sing with sweet voices, to eat with dainty appetites and manners, and to dance with grace. It is clear that Madame Edith, Father, Dame Olga, and even Hattie and Olive consider these important skills. These characters reinforce certain *stereotypes* that Ella confronts in her life.

Using specific examples from the text, write a paragraph that answers the following questions about the heroine of *Ella Enchanted*:

• How well does Ella acquire the "feminine" accomplishments described above?

• What value does she place on these skills?

• How does Ella measure up to the stereotypes of "proper" feminine behavior? To what extent does she resemble the original Cinderella?

• What does Ella represent for readers today?

Focus Your Reading

Vocabulary Words to Know

Study the following words and definitions. You will meet these words in your reading. Be sure to jot down in your word journal any other unknown words from the reading.

catapult—to hurl or launch

toiling—laboring; struggling

protruded—stuck out

perplexity—confusion; bewilderment

rapturous—ecstatic; carried away with emotion

irrefutable—unquestionable; not open to argument

grudgingly—reluctantly; unwillingly

endeavor—to strive; to try

besotted—madly in love; infatuated

solicitude—concern; anxiety

Things to Know

Here is some background information about this section of the book.

Wealthy women in earlier times often wore **wigs** to cover hair that was too thin for the elaborate hairstyles that were in fashion. Wigs were also commonly worn to cover hair that was dirty and unhygienic, since hair was not washed frequently. In addition, women wore **corsets,** close-fitting undergarments that were often lined with bone for support ("stays"). The corset was laced tightly around a woman's torso to make her look as slender as possible. When laced too tightly, a corset could actually make breathing difficult.

Bandits were a common hazard in the Middle Ages. These outlaws often preyed on travelers, attacking them on the road and robbing them. Travelers who could afford to do so journeyed by coach, with male servants riding on the outside for protection.

Focus Your Reading

Questions to Think About

The following questions will help you understand the meaning of what you read. You do not have to write out the answers to these questions. Instead, look at them before you begin reading, and think about them while you are reading.

1. As Ella rides with Sir Stephan, what information does he give about Char?

2. In what ways do the giants differ from the ogres? What skills do Ella and the other humans use in dealing with each group?

3. How does Ella try to trick Lucinda into ending the "blessing" she gave to Ella at birth?

4. How is the character of Ella's father further revealed as the story unfolds?

5. How has Ella been affected by the many changes in her life since her mother's death?

Build Your Vocabulary

Read the sentences below. On the line, write your definition of the word in bold type. Then, on another sheet of paper, use that word in a new sentence of your own.

1. "My heart began to pound so hard I thought it would **catapult** me backward off the horse."
   catapult: _____

2. " '**Toiling** knights are also diplomats,' I said."
   toiling: _____

3. "Uaaxee returned with a hamper from which **protruded** a chicken wing as big as a turkey."
   protruded: _____

4. "Some struggled with knives and forks the size of axes and shovels, some stared at their meal in **perplexity**."
   perplexity: _____

5. "The two plain ones were smiling, but the beautiful one was **rapturous**."
   rapturous: _____

6. " 'Your logic is **irrefutable**, although its foundation isn't sound.' "
   irrefutable: _____

7. " 'He sounds nice enough,' she said **grudgingly**."
   grudgingly: _____

8. " 'We shall stay here together, and you must all **endeavor** to lighten my desolation when my husband is away.' "
   endeavor: _____

9. "A blush deepened the color in her rouged cheeks. She was **besotted** with him."
   besotted: _____

10. "He was all **solicitude**, all tender attention."
    solicitude: _____

Check Your Understanding

Multiple Choice

Circle the letter of the best answer to each question.

1. When Ella and Sir Stephan travel together, how many days does he think it will take to arrive at the giant's wedding?
   a. three
   b. four
   c. five

2. What does the first giant say when Ella tells him that Uaaxee is not expecting her at the wedding?
   a. He says that he will run ahead to warn Uaaxee that Ella is arriving.
   b. He says that Uaaxee only allows guests who have been invited.
   c. He says that giants love strangers and that Uaaxee will thank Ella for coming.

3. How tall is Uaaxee?
   a. about twice as tall as a human
   b. about three times as tall as a human
   c. about four times as tall as a human

4. What "gift" does Lucinda give to the wedding couple at Uaaxee's farm?
   a. She says they will obey each other.
   b. She says they will never argue.
   c. She says they will always be together.

5. While talking to Lucinda, why does Ella feel as if her curse is really a blessing?
   a. She understands Lucinda's advice to be happy about it as a command.
   b. Ella realizes how lucky she is not to have been turned into a squirrel.
   c. She sees that Uaaxee's daughter has received a worse curse.

6. When Father and Ella speak at the wedding, how does he plan to become rich again?
   a. by marrying Ella off to a wealthy man
   b. by getting married to Dame Olga
   c. by selling Ella's mother's necklace

7. How does Ella describe the appearance of Edmund, Earl of Wolleck?
   a. like a walrus with a long mustache
   b. like a sad-eyed greyhound.
   c. like an old woman

8. How does the earl think that bandits should be punished?
   a. He thinks they should be treated harshly, perhaps even put to death.
   b. He thinks they should be banished from the kingdom.
   c. He thinks they should be shown mercy.

9. Why does Father tell the earl that he cannot marry Ella?
   a. He finds out the earl has little money.
   b. He believes Ella is too young and the earl too old.
   c. He feels guilty about tricking Ella.

10. What "gift" does Lucinda bestow on Father and Dame Olga at their wedding?
    a. to have all the riches they desire
    b. to love each other as long as they live
    c. to grow old together and never separate

Check Your Understanding

Short Answer

Write a short answer for each question.

1. What opinion does Sir Stephan have of Char? What examples does he give to back up this opinion?

2. Why does Ella cry after reading the story about Aladdin?

3. What clue does Ella look for in the crowd of wedding guests to figure out who Lucinda is?

4. What do the wedding couple pantomime together?

5. What does Father do when Ella tells him that she has run away from school?

6. Why does Mandy substitute regular mushrooms for the elvish ones that Father has ordered?

7. Why would Hattie's friend Blossom be troubled by Ella's marriage to the Earl of Wolleck?

8. How does Ella respond when the earl says that she is a child?

9. Why does Father want to avoid having his wedding in the manor house?

10. Why does Ella want to avoid Lucinda at her father's wedding to Dame Olga?

Deepen Your Understanding

Ella's magic book from Mandy often shows letters and journal entries written by other characters in the book. Sometimes these entries reveal valuable information that Ella can use to her advantage. At other times, an entry paints a clearer picture of a particular character.

Find one letter or journal entry that Ella has read in her magic book. Then respond in writing to the following questions:

• Why do you think the author has chosen to include this entry in the novel?

• How does this entry affect Ella? How does it affect the development of the story as a whole?

• Why has the author used the magic book as a device to reveal important information in the story? How effective is this?

Focus Your Reading

Vocabulary Words to Know

Study the following words and definitions. You will meet these words in your reading. Be sure to jot down in your word journal any other unknown words from the reading.

reticule—a small drawstring bag in which a woman could carry personal items

impertinent—improper; nosy

subterfuge—a plan designed to conceal something; deception

scruples—feelings of uneasiness about whether something is honorable or proper

servitude—the condition of lacking liberty, especially in deciding one's course in life

unguents—healing ointments

squalor—filthiness

cogitation—intense thought

heinous—shockingly bad; outrageous

artifice—trickiness; cleverness

Things to Know

Here is some background information about this section of the book.

A **doublet** was a tight-fitting jacket worn by men in Europe during the late Middle Ages and Renaissance.

Several types of dance are mentioned in this section of the book. The **gavotte** has a fairly fast pace; it comes from French folk tradition and involves high steps rather than sliding the feet. The **sarabande** is a slower, more formal dance similar to a minuet; it was often danced at court balls. A **courante** is a dance of Italian origin; it is fast-paced, requiring running steps. An **allemande,** originally a German folk dance, involves dancing at a moderate pace with linked arms. A **pavane** is a slow, stately court dance.

Focus Your Reading

Questions to Think About

The following questions will help you understand the meaning of what you read. You do not have to write out the answers to these questions. Instead, look at them before you begin reading, and think about them while you are reading.

1. How does Ella's relationship with Char continue to develop, both when they are together and when they are apart?

2. How is Ella affected by her father's marriage to Dame Olga?

3. In what ways does Ella continue to resist the control that Hattie, Olive, and Mum Olga have over her?

4. In how many ways does Mandy play the role of "fairy godmother" in Ella's life? How would life change for Ella if Mandy were not there?

5. How well (or poorly) does Sir Peter fulfill his duties as a father? How does this affect Ella?

Build Your Vocabulary

Read the sentences below. On the line, write your definition of the word in bold type. Then, on another sheet of paper, use that word in a new sentence of your own.

1. "She reached across the coach and pawed at me, ripping my **reticule** from my waist. . . . She dumped its contents on her lap."
   reticule: _____

2. " 'I have many questions, most of them **impertinent.**' "
   impertinent: _____

3. " 'You are shocked that I have proposed a **subterfuge.**' "
   subterfuge: _____

4. " 'My only hope is that one who flies down a stair rail as beautifully as you do can overcome his **scruples** in this matter.' "
   scruples: _____

5. "Midmorning of my second day of **servitude,** Olive joined us in the kitchen."
   servitude: _____

6. "As soon as she saw me, she rushed to her store of herbs and **unguents** and to the jug of Tonic."
   unguents: _____

7. "I think they gloried in my **squalor** as proof of my baseness."
   squalor: _____

8. " 'But, exhausted by his **cogitation,** he'd have energy left for only one word, the name of the flower.' "
   cogitation: _____

9. " 'Your crime: too much zeal in the protection of those you love. A fault and a virtue. **Heinous!**' "
   heinous: _____

10. " 'But I suppose that's the way with such women: They wouldn't be minxes if they weren't masters of **artifice** and fraud.' "
    artifice: _____

Check Your Understanding

Multiple Choice

Circle the letter of the best answer to each question.

1. On the day of her father's wedding, where does Ella hide from Lucinda?
   a. in the library behind closed doors
   b. outside beneath the candle trees
   c. in a dark corridor upstairs

2. Where do Char and Ella find the slippers?
   a. inside a stone bench
   b. underneath the spiral staircase
   c. in a corner of the upstairs terrace

3. What happens when Char comes to visit Ella on the day after the wedding?
   a. Hattie orders Ella to stay in her room.
   b. Olive and Hattie fight over Char.
   c. Dame Olga tells Char to go away.

4. What does Char write about Hattie's teeth?
   a. They are as small as a child's.
   b. They are the biggest he has ever seen.
   c. They are broken and crooked.

5. Why is Ella so reluctant to work as the laundress's helper?
   a. She does not want chapped hands.
   b. She has seen the laundress give a housemaid a black eye.
   c. The laundress will try to steal Ella's magic book and her silver KJs.

6. How does Ella get back at Mum Olga for making her scrub the floor?
   a. She puts an herb in her dinner that makes her fall asleep.
   b. She dumps a pail of dirty water over Mum Olga just before the guests arrive.
   c. She hangs her wig from the turret.

7. Why does Ella write her father after Mum Olga's formal dinner?
   a. She wants her father to find Char in Ayortha and bring him home to Kyrria.
   b. She wants her father to come home and save her from being a servant.
   c. She has important trading information about the elves.

8. What serious flaw does Char admit he has in one of his letters to Ella?
   a. He is slow to anger and slow to forgive.
   b. He is quick to anger yet quick to forgive.
   c. He is quick to anger and slow to forgive.

9. Why does Ella write a letter to Char that she pretends is from Hattie?
   a. Ella wants Char to think she eloped.
   b. Ella tries to amuse Char by making fun of Hattie's writing style.
   c. Ella and Hattie try to trick Char to discover which of them he prefers.

10. What does Mandy trick Lucinda into doing after she calls the fairy to her room?
    a. She gets Lucinda to end Ella's curse.
    b. She persuades her to banish Hattie and Olive from Kyrria.
    c. She makes her turn herself into a squirrel.

Check Your Understanding

Short Answer

Write a short answer for each question.

1. How do Char and Ella mark their trail in the old castle as they search for the secret passageway?

2. Why is Char planning to spend a year living at the court of Ayortha?

3. What do Father, Mum Olga, and the rest of Ella's new family see Ella and Char doing?

4. When Ella writes to Char, how does she tell him to address any letters to her?

5. What does Mum Olga do to Ella as soon as Father leaves home for his business trip?

6. What things does Olive demand of Ella on Ella's second day as a servant?

7. Where is the safest place in the house for Ella to hide from Olive? Why?

8. What does Char reveal to Ella in his letter dated Thursday, May 24?

9. Why does Ella decide that she must convince Char to give her up?

10. Why does Mandy summon Lucinda to her room to speak with her?

Deepen Your Understanding

Many fairy tales include a character known as a "fairy godmother." This magical person is usually described as being beautiful and dainty; she always manages to make things come out right for the "damsel in distress," or the heroine of the fairy tale.

In *Ella Enchanted,* Mandy is Ella's fairy godmother. Mandy has watched carefully over Ella's grandmother, Ella's mother, and now Ella herself, since their births.

Respond in writing to the following questions, using specific examples from the novel:

• In what ways is Mandy a "standard" fairy godmother?

• In what ways is Mandy not a usual fairy godmother?

• How does Mandy affect the plot development of *Ella Enchanted?* How does she affect the well-being of Ella, the novel's heroine?

Focus Your Reading

Vocabulary Words to Know

Study the following words and definitions. You will meet these words in your reading. Be sure to jot down in your word journal any other unknown words from the reading.

proximity—closeness; the state of being nearby

desolate—joyless; gloomy; lonely

edicts—commands; official orders

incantations—spells or charms that are recited out loud

sovereign—supreme ruler

pastoral—dealing with the simple charms of country life

tedium—boredom

covert—hidden; secret

corrosive—able to weaken or destroy by wearing away

chicanery—trickery; deception

Things to Know

Here is some background information about this section of the book.

A **carpetbag** was a kind of traveler's luggage often used in earlier eras. It was made of tapestry or thin carpet fabric.

An **epilogue** is a special section that comes at the end of a novel or play. It serves as a conclusion to the story that has just been told. Sometimes an epilogue is a general commentary on the situation of the characters and events just described. At other times, it tells what happens to the main characters at a later point in time.

Focus Your Reading

Questions to Think About

The following questions will help you understand the meaning of what you read. You do not have to write out the answers to these questions. Instead, look at them before you begin reading, and think about them while you are reading.

1. Why is Ella so angry with Mandy after Lucinda's second visit to Mandy's room?

2. Even though she doesn't want Char to recognize her, and Mum Olga will not allow her to go, why does Ella decide to attend the three balls?

3. How do Mandy and Lucinda distinguish between "big magic" and "small magic"?

4. How does Ella capture the attention of Prince Charmont at the first ball? How does she maintain his interest at the next two balls?

5. What finally enables Ella to escape the burden of her curse?

Build Your Vocabulary

Read the sentences below. On the line, write your definition of the word in bold type. Then, on another sheet of paper, use that word in a new sentence of your own.

1. "Within, noblemen in my **proximity** would beg me to dance."
   proximity: _____

2. " 'I shall be **desolate** if you don't remember me, Prince,' she cooed at her reflection."
   desolate: _____

3. "I soaked away a year of cinders and grime and Mum Olga's orders and Hattie's **edicts** and Olive's demands."
   edicts: _____

4. "She muttered no **incantations,** waved no wand."
   incantations: _____

5. "I had been here before, as a week-old infant brought to meet my **sovereign,** but not since."
   sovereign: _____

6. "Every wall was covered with tapestries: hunting scenes, court scenes, **pastoral** scenes."
   pastoral: _____

7. "I'm pleased to have found a friend at these balls, where I expected to find only **tedium.**"
   tedium: _____

8. "I was the cause of his joy and would be the cause of his destruction: . . . a **covert** signal given by me, poison in his glass, a dagger in his ribs, a fall from a parapet."
   covert: _____

9. "My mouth filled with liquid, bile and blood from biting my tongue, salty and **corrosive** and sweet."
   corrosive: _____

10. "Char watched over him and intervened when necessary to save him or his victims from the consequences of his **chicanery.**"
    chicanery: _____

Check Your Understanding

Multiple Choice

Circle the letter of the best answer to each question.

1. When Mandy summons Lucinda to her room for the second time, how does Lucinda look to Ella?
   a. old and wrinkled
   b. young and radiant
   c. tired and sad

2. How does Ella find the dresses to wear to the three royal balls?
   a. She wears old dresses of her mother's that Mandy has altered.
   b. Lucinda magically makes new ones.
   c. Mandy finds dresses that Hattie has thrown out and alters them for Ella.

3. When Char meets Ella disguised at the first ball, why does he think they met before?
   a. Her eyes look familiar to him through the mask.
   b. When he takes her hand, it feels familiar.
   c. He recognizes her laugh.

4. What does Char sing for Ella at the second royal ball?
   a. an Ayorthaian mourning song
   b. an Ayorthaian homecoming song
   c. a Kyrrian wedding song

5. Where has Mandy found the tiara and necklace that Ella wears to the third ball?
   a. at the market
   b. in a trunk that belonged to Ella's mother
   c. in a package from Lucinda

6. What does Hattie tell the disguised Ella during the third ball?
   a. Prince Charmont is secretly engaged to Ella of Frey.
   b. Dame Olga is the wealthiest woman in Kyrria.
   c. Hattie is secretly engaged to Prince Charmont.

7. What does Mandy do when Ella returns and tells her that she has endangered Char and Kyrria?
   a. Mandy tells Ella to pack her things and prepare to leave.
   b. Mandy tells Ella she should marry Char.
   c. Mandy tells Lucinda to break the spell.

8. How does Ella respond when Char asks why she won't marry him?
   a. She tells him that she would never make a good princess.
   b. She tells him that she is cursed.
   c. She says that she is already engaged.

9. After Char and Ella become engaged, how much time passes before their marriage?
   a. one year
   b. six months
   c. one month

10. Who is *not* invited to Ella and Char's wedding?
    a. Ella's father
    b. Uaaxee
    c. Lucinda

Check Your Understanding

Short Answer

Write a short answer for each question.

1. After Lucinda returns from her experiences as a squirrel and an obedient child, why does she still tell Ella that she cannot help her?

2. According to Areida's journal, what are the two ways in which she has contradicted Prince Charmont?

3. What does Ella say her bath water is like when her servant is also her fairy godmother?

4. How does the disguised Ella introduce herself to Prince Charmont at the ball?

5. Why does Ella feel that the damsel with the yellow hair is a "rival"?

6. Why does Prince Charmont find Lady Lela's carriage so unusual?

7. What does Queen Daria tell the disguised Ella after she searches her face at the third ball?

8. What makes King Jerrold frown while he talks to Lady Lela at the ball?

9. What clues make Ella realize that her curse has finally been broken?

10. What does Ella choose to be called instead of "Princess"?

Deepen Your Understanding

"I was made anew. Ella. Just Ella. Not Ella, the slave. Not a scullery maid. Not Lela. Not Eleanor. Ella. Myself unto myself. One. Me."

—*Chapter Twenty-Nine*

In the final chapter of *Ella Enchanted,* the main character sums herself up in the words quoted above. She has gained new insights about herself and others. She has tackled many challenges to achieve this new sense of identity and confidence. In novels, this kind of progression is called *character development.*

How does this novel tell the story of Ella's journey from childhood innocence to adult maturity? Give specific examples from the text that show key moments in Ella's personal growth.

End-of-Book Test

Circle the letter of the best answer to each question.

1. How old is Ella when her mother dies?
   a. nearly fifteen
   b. twelve
   c. five

2. How much older than Ella is Prince Charmont?
   a. one year
   b. two years
   c. three years

3. What does Hattie tell Ella at the reception after the funeral of Ella's mother?
   a. Ella should come to finishing school and learn some manners.
   b. Ella's father is not rich enough for Hattie's mother.
   c. Ella's mother was ill-bred.

4. How does Mandy respond when Ella first asks her to break Lucinda's spell?
   a. She says that it is impossible for anyone but Lucinda to break the spell.
   b. She says that no one has broken a fairy's spell before.
   c. She says that she knows it can be done, but she does not know how.

5. What does Char say to Ella when he meets her at the royal menagerie?
   a. He says that he should not be talking to her while she is in mourning.
   b. He says that he will be going to battle.
   c. He says that he likes her.

6. What luggage does Ella take to school?
   a. one trunk and a barrel of Tonic
   b. two trunks and a barrel of Tonic
   c. three trunks and a barrel of Tonic

7. In what sort of building is Madame Edith's finishing school?
   a. in a medium-sized stone manor
   b. in a small castle with turrets
   c. in an ordinary wooden house

8. What does Ella like to imagine when she goes to bed at night at Madame Edith's?
   a. She likes to think about Char and the adventures they might go on together.
   b. She thinks about all of the things she would do if her curse were broken.
   c. She pretends that she is a beautiful, graceful princess with perfect manners.

9. What does Char write to his father about Ella's being at finishing school?
   a. He hopes that she will be able to develop her talent for languages there.
   b. He fears it will have a bad effect on her.
   c. He admires her for meeting new people.

10. What compliment does the elf woman who meets Ella give her?
    a. She says that Ella is lovely under the dirt of her journey.
    b. She says that Ella speaks Elfian well.
    c. She says that Ella is not like her father.

(continued)

End-of- Book Test (continued)

11. Why does Slannen say he is happy to give Ella the stirrup cup?
    a. The elves like to give their best pieces to people who love them.
    b. Ella's father treated him generously.
    c. The elves are impressed by Ella's efforts to speak their language.

12. How does Char react when Ella describes her finishing school "accomplishments"?
    a. He is worried that Ella might actually be proud of these new skills.
    b. He is delighted to see that Ella is no longer as clumsy as a small elephant.
    c. He says that he would like to hire the Manners Mistress to work at the palace.

13. How does Ella respond when Uaaxee says that she will tell Sir Peter that his daughter has come to the wedding?
    a. Ella asks Uaaxee not to tell her father; she wants to surprise him.
    b. Ella thanks Uaaxee for helping; she wants to rest and eat while Uaaxee fetches her father.
    c. Ella goes with Uaaxee to meet him.

14. How has Sir Peter lost his money?
    a. The elves' pottery factory he invested in burned to the ground.
    b. He was robbed by a trader from Ayortha.
    c. He was caught selling an estate he didn't own.

15. When Sir Peter is forced to dismiss the servants, why does he not dismiss Mandy?
    a. He is afraid of her magical power.
    b. She is such a good cook.
    c. He knows she can best care for Ella.

16. When Father sells off their possessions, what do Mandy and Ella hide?
    a. Mother's jewels
    b. Mother's favorite chair
    c. the fairy rug

17. When Mum Olga says that Ella will have to earn her keep, what does Father answer?
    a. He agrees with his new wife that Ella should work and respect her elders.
    b. He says that if Ella must become a servant to save the family money, so must Hattie and Olive.
    c. He says that Ella must not be a servant in her own house.

18. How does Mandy rescue Ella from working for the laundress?
    a. She persuades Dame Olga to let Ella be a housemaid for Hattie instead.
    b. She tells Dame Olga that she needs Ella to be her scullery maid.
    c. She reminds Dame Olga that Sir Peter will not allow Ella to be a servant.

19. Why does Ella think she cannot marry Char?
    a. She is no longer a lady; she is a servant.
    b. Her curse will be a danger to him.
    c. Mum Olga will never allow it.

20. How is Ella's curse finally broken?
    a. Ella breaks it herself when she loves Char enough to resist marrying him.
    b. Mandy and Lucinda secretly agree to do one last bit of "big magic."
    c. Ella breaks the curse after Char's orders.

I. CHAPTERS ONE–FIVE

Build Your Vocabulary

Wording and definitions may vary. Students may remember the definitions given in the Vocabulary Words to Know section of Focus Your Reading or may refine the definitions based on the context and the reading overall. Students' new sentences will vary.

Check Your Understanding: Multiple Choice

1. b		6. b
2. a		7. a
3. c		8. a
4. b		9. c
5. c		10. c

Check Your Understanding: Short Answer

1. Ella learns about the curse at her fifth birthday party. She cannot stop eating cake after Mandy hands her a slice and says, "Eat."
2. She remembers the times when she and her mother have slid down the banister together.
3. He hugs her, but only to muffle the noise of her crying. Then he tells her to go away until she can calm herself down.
4. She catches her skirt in the door of the carriage and rips it. Char laughs.
5. Her ears buzz, the floor seems to tilt, and she feels as if she will fly into a thousand pieces.
6. She says that he was poor when he married Lady Eleanor, but that he ended up making her richer.
7. She learns that Mandy is her fairy godmother.
8. Her feet haven't grown for a few years; fairies have tiny feet.
9. She says that although she doesn't know how to do it, it can be done.
10. He reminds her of a carnival toy—a leather fist at the end of a coiled spring.

Deepen Your Understanding

Answers will vary but may include some of the following ideas:
- The lines refer to a *fairy* and a *curse;* this signals to the reader that the novel will be a fantasy. It also introduces the narrator's dilemma: the unintentional problems caused by Lucinda's "gift."
- The first words ("That fool of a fairy Lucinda") introduce an informal, conversational tone. This is also a first-person narrative, indicating a fairly personal tale. The sentences are short and direct—honest and plain-spoken, like Ella herself.

II. CHAPTERS SIX–TEN

Build Your Vocabulary

Wording and definitions may vary. Students may remember the definitions given in the Vocabulary Words to Know section of Focus Your Reading, or they may refine the definitions based on the context and the reading overall. Students' new sentences will vary.

Check Your Understanding: Multiple Choice

1. c		6. b
2. c		7. a
3. b		8. c
4. a		9. a
5. a		10. c

Check Your Understanding: Short Answer

1. Creatures in the royal menagerie include a hydra, a baby dragon, exotics (a unicorn, centaurs, and gryphons), talking parrots, and ogres.
2. Ogres are big and cruel. They also can know your secrets just by looking at you, and they can speak so persuasively that it is irresistible—like being under a spell.
3. He commands Ella to stop.
4. Ella picks it up, then grinds it into Hattie's face.
5. She gives Olive money, as requested (one silver KJ).
6. Hattie lets Ella drink Tonic because Hattie has already tried it and found it revolting; she only wants to keep Ella from eating and drinking good things.
7. The coachman slaps Olive across the face.
8. Her dress is stained and wrinkled, and her hair is probably a mess.
9. They speak in Ayorthaian, which no one else understands.
10. He has brought her a centaur colt.

Deepen Your Understanding

Answers will vary.

III. CHAPTERS ELEVEN–FIFTEEN

Build Your Vocabulary

Wording and definitions may vary. Students may remember the definitions given in the Vocabulary Words to Know section of Focus Your Reading, or they may refine the definitions based on the context and the reading overall. Students' new sentences will vary.

Check Your Understanding: Multiple Choice

1. c	6. a
2. a	7. b
3. c	8. c
4. a	9. c
5. b	10. a

Check Your Understanding: Short Answer

1. She does not like them much, nor do they like her. Her only true friend is Areida.
2. It makes her cry, which brings Ella some relief.
3. If they can sing and dance charmingly, eat daintily, and sew a little, they will be fine ladies, according to Dame Olga.
4. She hopes to find Lucinda there and ask her to take back her "blessing."
5. He draws a map in flour on the pastry board.
6. She is happy to have escaped from school; she feels completely free.
7. The elves can tell by looking into Ella's eyes that she is kind; she also speaks to them in Elfian.
8. She can't escape because NiSSh has ordered her not to run away.
9. One of the knights has been acting as a scout and has seen Ella talking the ogres into sleep.
10. After reprimanding the ogres, Ella smiles at Char. Her smile makes him blush.

Deepen Your Understanding

Answers will vary, although student responses should include at least some of the following ideas:
- Ella manages to acquire all of the ladylike skills she is taught (except penmanship) because all of her teachers (except Writing Mistress) order her to do so.
- She has no interest in these skills and places little value on them—with the exception of writing, which she admits can be useful.
- Unlike the original Cinderella, an example of obedience, Ella only obeys because she must. At heart, she is a rebel. She is independent and brave and has a great curiosity about the wider world.
- Her attitude sets her apart from her schoolmates and "modernizes" Ella; she is a democratic, self-reliant young woman with keen intelligence and a will of her own.

IV. CHAPTERS SIXTEEN–TWENTY

Build Your Vocabulary

Wording and definitions may vary. Students may remember the definitions given in the Vocabulary Words to Know section of Focus Your Reading, or they may refine the definitions based on the context and the reading overall. Students' new sentences will vary.

Check Your Understanding: Multiple Choice

1. a	6. a
2. c	7. b
3. b	8. c
4. c	9. a
5. a	10. b

Check Your Understanding: Short Answer

1. Sir Stephan thinks that Char is wonderful: eager and quick to learn, kind (as shown when Char helps the fruit-and-vegetable seller pick up his produce), smart, and steady. But Char doesn't play enough and may be too serious (he has laughed more with Ella in one morning than in two weeks with his knights and councilors).
2. She cries because, like the genie in the story, she is not free.
3. She looks for tiny fairy feet in the crowd.
4. They pantomime their life together: planting corn, building a house, having children and grandchildren, and dying.
5. He laughs with pride at her courage.
6. She is trying to prevent Ella from eating the elvish mushrooms because they will make Ella fall in love with her father's dinner guest.
7. The Earl is Blossom's uncle; Blossom is to inherit his money if he does not marry.

8. She says that she is not a child and that her mother married at sixteen. If she were to die young, she would rather have lived and loved.

9. He doesn't want Dame Olga to see that all of the furnishings have been sold because he has lost his money.

10. She doesn't want Lucinda to see her; Lucinda would realize that Ella deceived her when they met at the giant's wedding.

Deepen Your Understanding

Answers will vary.

V. Chapters Twenty-One–Twenty-Five

Build Your Vocabulary

Wording and definitions may vary. Students may remember the definitions given in the Vocabulary Words to Know section of Focus Your Reading, or they may refine the definitions based on the context and the reading overall. Students' new sentences will vary.

Check Your Understanding: Multiple Choice

1. c	6. a
2. a	7. b
3. a	8. a
4. b	9. a
5. b	10. c

Check Your Understanding: Short Answer

1. Char pulls the buttons off his doublet and uses them as trail markers.

2. The future ruler of Kyrria always spends a long period at the court of Ayortha, and vice versa. This keeps the peace between the two nations.

3. They see Ella slide down the banister into Char's arms.

4. She tells him to address the letters to Mandy.

5. She moves Ella into a "cell" of a room in the servants' quarters. She makes Ella a servant.

6. She asks for a white cake, she asks Ella to talk and tell stories, she asks for water, and she asks for money.

7. It is safe to hide in the library, because neither Hattie nor Olive cares for books.

8. Char says that he loves Ella. He has loved her since the first time they met at her mother's funeral. He wants to marry her.

9. She realizes that her curse makes her dangerous. People could take advantage of her, hurting Char and Kyrria in the process.

10. She decides that Lucinda must experience the kinds of "blessings" she gives to others. She tricks Lucinda into turning herself into a squirrel and an obedient child.

Deepen Your Understanding

Answers will vary. Student responses should include at least some of the following observations:

• Mandy is a "standard" fairy godmother in that she loves Ella and tries to help and protect her. She gives Ella some supernatural "tools" (Tonic, the magic story book) to help her ward off various ills and navigate life with success. She also keeps Ella under her wing after Sir Peter marries Dame Olga and Ella is reduced to a servant.

• Mandy is not a typical fairy godmother in that she isn't radiantly beautiful like Lucinda (Mandy has "frizzy gray hair in disarray" and a "double chin"). She also refuses to use "big magic" to help Ella out of her predicaments. (When Ella attends the ball in the rain, it is Lucinda who conjures up the pumpkin-coach with all its trappings. Mandy simply hands Ella an umbrella.) Moreover, Mandy is not always able to fix things that have gone wrong (she does not know how to undo Lucinda's curse; she can't keep Sir Peter from serving the elvish mushrooms at dinner).

• Mandy affects the plot as a character with a supporting role. She helps the plot along indirectly as an information provider—telling Ella important information about the fairy world, giving Ella the magic book, and so on. She plays a more direct role in curbing the effects of Lucinda's clumsy magic—by tricking Lucinda into learning what obedience really means. Mandy affects Ella's well-being by becoming Ella's surrogate mother after Lady Eleanor dies. Even more important than her magical power is her love of Ella and her comfort and support in times of trouble. She encourages Ella to think for herself and to discover her own inner strength to overcome all obstacles, including breaking the curse.

VI. CHAPTERS TWENTY-SIX–EPILOGUE

Build Your Vocabulary

Wording and definitions may vary. Students may remember the definitions given in the Vocabulary Words to Know section of Focus Your Reading, or they may refine the definitions based on the context and the reading overall. Students' new sentences will vary.

Check Your Understanding: Multiple Choice

1. a	6. c
2. a	7. a
3. b	8. b
4. b	9. c
5. a	10. c

Check Your Understanding: Short Answer

1. Lucinda says that she has given up big magic forever; ending Ella's curse would be big magic.
2. Areida tells Char that Ella doesn't care about money; she doesn't think that Ella has changed.
3. The water never gets cold or dirty, and you never get scalded. You get sparkling clean.
4. Ella introduces herself as Lela from Bast.
5. Ella considers her a rival because the blond damsel makes Char laugh at the first ball. He also dances with her three times at the second ball.
6. He thinks that it is an unusual color (orange).
7. The queen tells Ella that, despite the mask, Ella reminds her of a lady she admired who had very playful spirits.
8. The king frowns at Ella's mask. Most take their masks off when they speak to the king or queen.
9. Ella disobeys several orders, yet has none of the usual symptoms: she tells Char she won't marry him; she refuses to marry Char and give Olive her money; she doesn't go to her room; she tells Char she is cursed.
10. She takes the titles of Court Linguist and Cook's Helper.

Deepen Your Understanding

Answers will vary, but student responses should include at least some of the following ideas:
- Ella first discovers the meaning of Lucinda's curse on her fifth birthday; she begins to realize the danger it can put her in. She also learns that she has a fairy godmother. At the age of eight, Ella tells her friend, Pamela, about the curse. After experiencing the negative consequences, she promises her mother never to tell anyone again. ("I had learned caution.")
- When she is nearly fifteen, Ella's mother dies. Ella meets Char, learns that Mandy is her fairy godmother, and begins to see her father more clearly—and to dislike what she sees. With Mandy's help, she begins to accept her mother's death.
- At finishing school, Ella has her first true friend and experiences the pain of giving her up. She performs as required at school, but secretly rebels against the silly traditions. She becomes more independent, which leads to her running away.
- On her journey to Uaaxee's farm, Ella continues her transition to adulthood. She is happy on her own and approaches each new experience with intelligence and daring (making friends with the elves, lulling the ogres to sleep, finding Lucinda at the wedding). At her father's wedding reception, Ella isolates herself from her new family; she has her own identity and values. She dances with Char and begins to fall in love.
- After Ella is made a servant by her stepmother, she learns restraint (by not telling Char about the curse, even though she is miserable) and bravery (she does not cry or become weak, despite the abuse she receives).
- Although Ella loves Char deeply, she will not marry him because it would put him—and the country—at risk. Ella has matured enough to be able to love another human being more than herself. Her generosity and willingness to sacrifice her own feelings to protect Char and Kyrria are what, in fact, break the spell. She is capable of adult emotions and actions.

END-OF-BOOK TEST

1. a	11. a
2. b	12. a
3. c	13. a
4. c	14. c
5. c	15. b
6. a	16. c
7. c	17. c
8. b	18. b
9. b	19. b
10. c	20. a